The Hidden Nugget Revealed

A New Sound Declares God's Glory in Creation

Dr. C. Patrica Noble

2024

THE HIDDEN NUGGET REVEALED: A New Sound Declares God's Glory in Creation

ISBN: 978-976-97243-2-7 (paperback) 978-976-97243-3-4 (ebook)

Quotations and scriptures are taken from the New King James, New International and King James Version of the Bible.

Editor: Lana Evans

Photography by: Smartshag Photography

Book Cover Design: Sylvia M Dallas

Published by: The Publisher's Notebook Limited

2024

Endorsements

Pastor Caren Morrison
Senior Pastor, Fellowship Tabernacle Portmore

A great eye opener to the works and worth of Reggae music and dance as an acceptable form of worship to God. This book is a must have in your collection. If you are struggling with whether or not Reggae is of God, then you simply must get a copy of this book. If you love gospel Reggae, grab this book. If you are still alive on the face of this earth, this book is a must have.

While reading, I experienced moments of joy and victory with an increased passion for the ministry of Reggae music and dance. A self-acclaimed dancer; just give me that reggae beat and my body immediately goes into motion. I love all genres of music but Reggae is by far my all time favourite.

This book also reveals the thrilling history and background to Reggae music in the church in Jamaica.

This is one of those books that once you start reading, you don't want to put it down. Interestingly, I never knew I was included until I read the chapter written by my husband (I guess he wanted to surprise me knowing how much I love surprises).

I personally am very happy to see what the Lord has done through Aunty Pat and Praise Academy of Dance. She has availed herself to be used of God mightily for such a time as this. I wait with great anticipation for His next move for gospel Reggae and dance. Reggae is the musical language of Jamaicans, to be made the musical language of the world.

Anica Wood
Dancer / Marketing Consultant

This book delves into the dimensions of reggae and the vast influence it has on the lives of others especially when coupled with dance.

There are many skeptics of reggae being used as a form of worship. This is due to its reputation of having many songs with unethical/vulgar lyrical content. The author is not oblivious to secular types of this nature; her focus is rather on the type that focuses on the principles of God and those that can carry a powerful anointing.

Dr. Cynthia Patrica Noble has been involved in dance ministry for over 25 years. She has a sincere passion for the Lord and worship. As a pioneer of Christian dance ministry, she has witnessed time again, the transformational effects that gospel reggae has on dancers and individuals on a whole. I believe this makes her more than qualified to give insight on the matters highlighted in The Hidden Nugget Revealed.

As a dancer, I have personally experienced the overwhelming power of the Holy Spirit while performing to gospel reggae. The music has an infectious nature and emits a sense of power. Having experienced miraculous breakthroughs while dancing, I can attest to the transformational effects of gospel reggae and dance which the author passionately speaks about.

Dr. Noble and I have had many discussions about the various signs and wonders we've both encountered while dancing. I've seen where she has documented some real-life experiences, so I have no doubt of this book's authenticity.

I endorse this book wholeheartedly as it will:

- recommend a viable option that can bring youths closer to Christ
- empower Christian dancers
- encourage the church to embrace gospel reggae and dance more
- provide insights on the positive influence of gospel reggae on society as a whole.
- educate readers who are skeptical about reggae as a form of worship
- enlighten those who don't believe that dance is appropriate for worship
- Psalms 150: 4
- "Praise him with the timbrel and dance: praise him with stringed instruments and organs."

Dacia Miller
Dancer, Praise Academy of Dance, Jamaica

As a dancer, with a keen interest and love for gospel reggae and gospel reggae dance, this book "The Hidden Nugget Revealed," written by Dr. Patrica Noble, serve as an eye opener.

It is insightful and inspiring to read about the events leading up to the revival that birthed gospel reggae in Jamaica. It really puts into perspective what many of us have come to know and understand as normal in the Christian circles highlighting its history.

Moreover, it really heightened my awareness to the prayers and desires of those who were committed and obedient to God's leading to bring forth such a powerful weapon for the Kingdom of God.

The testimonies of deliverance and freedom that this tool - gospel reggae dance, really sets my bones on fire to want to use this gift of dance for the transformation of lives in an effort to populate the kingdom of God.

What is even more outstanding, is that God has already started this gospel reggae dance movement within the Caribbean. My hope is that as individuals read this book spirits will be ignited and many more set ablaze for the Kingdom of God as the Lord of the dance continues to use gospel reggae dance, throughout the Caribbean region and spread right across the world.

DEDICATION

This book, 'The Hidden Nugget Revealed, is dedicated to all the persons who have a love for gospel reggae music and dance.

Its also for those who believe that it is more relevant in this season than ever before and can help to change our communal way of living as individuals and as a nation. Praise Academy of Dance, Jamaica and Barbados have opened the eyes of many persons locally and internationally to be able to accept and embrace these missing nuggets because of their fearless attitude.

I salute these dancers and choreographers as heroes because we broke all traditional barriers.

To all the Christian dance ministers and ministries who are embarking on this new path, be creative and 'Doan Watch Nuh Face'.

I give praises to God for those churches who have accepted and continue to use this genre in their praise and worship sessions. My prayer is that all pastors in our churches will realise how important it is to eliminate the stigma that reggae gospel music is not of God and embrace God's Word that all things were created for His glory.

To all the reggae gospel artistes who have been anointed by God to keep this genre of music going, I implore you to stay on the pathway of righteousness, holiness and integrity. Let excellence propel you and allow the Word of God to align and activate every word, sound and rhythm.

TABLE OF CONTENTS

Contents

CREATED WITH
IMAGINE

FOREWORD

My first encounter with this artistic woman of God was in her dance class at Jessie Ripoll Primary School in Jamaica in the mid-1980s. Having grown up with a deep love for the arts, particularly dancing, I wanted a way to express this love in a space that was "safe" and held true to my Christian values. Dr. Patrica Noble's dance class became that space.

Soon after, she moved the classes to the Covenant Community Church tent at 97 Old Hope Road under the name Praise Academy of Dance, and there I was with her. I was not aware of another environment like the one provided by her where persons of the Christian faith like me who had a passion for dancing could express their God given talent without fear of "condemnation".

Condemnation sounds like a strong term but that was the approach of the church to dance back then. Dancing was seen as of the world and as such Christians should not participate in such activities. Dr. Noble was bold enough to follow the leading of her God and Father, going against the dominant church culture, to redeem the dance and the reggae genre.

Forerunners, pioneers of great works are usually faced with opposition and skepticism from those who have established themselves as keepers of the tradition and Dr. Noble was no exception. As she danced to the rhythm of the Jamaican people, reggae, she was shunned by many of the leaders of the Christian church, yet she persevered, kept by the fire of the Holy Spirit locked deep in her belly and the vision of God's desire to do this new and unique thing in the realm of the dance.

Proverbs 20:5 says: "Counsel in the heart of man is like deep water; But a man of understanding will draw it out". Dr. Noble had the counsel of God in her heart as deep water and, praise God, she was a woman of understanding and drew it out as a sweet fragrance to so many of us.

Deeply rooted in the soul of the black man is the rhythm of its time. It was the cultural music and song that kept our forefathers and was a source of inspiration, enabling them to endure the ravishes of slavery. So to deny our music is to deny that which gives our people life and resilience, and which buoys our indomitable spirit as a people. God says in Acts 17: 26-27 that He marks out the boundaries of our lands such that people would seek Him and find Him. I am convinced that one medium used by God for the peoples of the Caribbean and Jamaica, in particular, is music and reggae is our music. Consequently, He will use it and has been using it for His praise and glory.

In this book Dr. Noble takes the lead again to demonstrate how God has been true to His word to her that He would do something different and unique through the dance coupled with the reggae genre. She speaks to the power of the genre to dismantle strongholds of oppression and to liberate the minds and souls of people; to tear down and dismantle strongholds and to build lasting and impactful structures in the lives of people, communities and nations.

The book further speaks of how God in his wisdom and sovereignty is using gospel reggae to redeem, reshape and restore that which the enemy of our souls, the devil, has sought to destroy.

This book is as informative as it is instructive. It will challenge your perspective as it demonstrates the power of dance and gospel reggae music to change lives. The book makes a good and potent read.

Professor Shermaine Barrett (PhD), Chair, Praise Academy of Dance

ACKNOWLEDGMENTS

Thanks to The Trinity. ..Father God, Jesus Christ The Son and The Holy Spirit for the instructions given to be able to write this book. The inspiration received enabled me to gain greater knowledge and confidence in the word of God and to understand how God created all things for His Glory.

To my beloved family; sisters - Norma, Monica, and Donna, my brother - Keith; nieces - Sharon, Stacey, Sacha, Andrea; nephews Ramon and Joniel who continue to believe in me and the talents that God has deposited in me. Your consistent support for me in all my endeavours since you discovered and accepted my creative skills have been tremendous and very heart warming. Blessings to you all.

My constant and genuine friends and pastors from the different church families who have always encouraged and motivated me, thank you.

The kind contributors, Pastor Courtney Morrison, Keisha Campbell, Patricia Cox - Praise Academy of Dance (Barbados), Patrick Kitson, founder for the Reggae Gospel

Band – CHANGE, who knowing the heart of a great God, and the missing nugget from the Church, didn't hesitate to respond confidently to the writing of this book.

To Dacia Miller, Anica Wood, Pastor Caren Morrison, and Professor Shermaine Barrett thank you for adding such incredible thoughts as you recommend this book for our ardent readers who I have no doubt will appreciate this missing nugget.

INTRODUCTION

God is revealing Himself more and more through the Arts which is becoming more visible and is impacting the lives of our children and youths in so many different ways. The Word of God is coming through different avenues in various creative ways especially since this new norm of life is bringing transformation in our homes, communities and nations. God wants us to forget the former things and embrace the new thing that He's doing - using a more practical method of delivery. He creates all music but not all music glorify Him. He's redeeming, reshaping, and restoring what the enemy destroyed.

With gospel reggae music comes the dance to enhance and deliver His word which not only provides entertainment, but it brings salvation, healing, and deliverance because of its visibility.

- Do you need a breakthrough from suicidal attempts, oppression, sexual immorality, fear, and intimidation?
- Have you discovered your talent to sing gospel reggae music and you're hiding your talent because you are fearful?
- Are you afraid to dance this type of music because you feel dance is not of God?

- Now is the time to break free from your fear and fulfill that long time passion and help to make a difference to this changing world.
- What COVID has done is not only to bring negativity to so many homes and lives, but it has also brought a positive side to it for us to realise that God's DNA is embedded in us for greater works.

The Hidden Nugget Revealed
A New Sound Declares God's Glory in Creation
Dr. C. Patrica Noble

Chapter 1

The Hidden Nugget Revealed

The Heartbeat of God

In my first book, entitled ***The Journey Continues...*** I explained the concept of reggae music coming from the heart of God to bring transformation to individuals, community and nation, hence the acronym:

R Redeemed from the hands of the enemy

E Energetic

G God-given

G Good

A Anointed

E Everlasting

This was my conversation with God:

God: *I'm introducing you, my daughter, to something different and unique.*

Daughter: *Why? This music is not good for the Church.*

God: *It's of Me and from Me; I just need a vessel to operate from. Many are waiting for this unique sound, and the dance is about to enhance this new move.*

What a chaotic and uncertain moment. Wow, talk about shock! That was me, Pat Noble. God assured me that many will not receive it at first but, because He created it, then it will come to fruition.

Reggae music comes with different facets: accents, rhythms, tones and energy. It's a different kind of music that makes you want to listen, need to listen; it keeps you moving. It can't be boring—just interesting. Since this music originated in the heart of God, then it cannot be ignored nor rejected. That's why even the children, people on the bus, the homeless person on the street, a jogger, someone on the beach, in a bar—once the music is being played the body responds with different movements from different sections of the body and these movements do not have to be repulsive or vulgar.

Reggae is being redeemed, not only in the gospel arena, but in every sector nationally or internationally and has been attracting different vibes. Many persons have become more accommodating and receptive, especially the Church who originally thought it was taboo. Owing to the changes in technology and with a new generation evolving, reggae gospel has found a more conducive environment to enhance its development.

The Anointing and The Youth

Reggae is a sound to penetrate the darkness and the evil that is destroying from the youngest to the oldest. The anointing on this type of music is exceptional in that most of the songs done by our gospel reggae artistes are derived from the Word of God and cultural elements.

Hebrews 4:12 speaks of the Word like this:

> *"For the word of God is living and powerful, and sharper than any two-edged sword, piercing even to the division of soul and spirit, and of joints and marrow, and is a discerner of the thoughts and intents of the heart."*

In Jeremiah chapter 20:9, it says:

> *"His word is in my heart like a fire, I'm weary of holding it in, indeed I cannot."*

There is a power that emanates from the Word of God, which is channeled by the artiste which makes the anointing greater.

An artiste who operated in the secular and comes to be a believer is more powerful in his/her delivery because the execution is being influenced through the Holy Spirit and the Word of God. With this kind of visibility, there will be many world changers. This new thrust in this type of music will provide our children and youths with a redeemed revolutionary culture which is of God, to change mindsets and beliefs.

Our younger generation will experience a more stable foundation where they will hear songs promoting more about:

a. the gospel message of Jesus Christ

b. righteous living

c. non-violence

d. love

e. peace

The churches, schools and tertiary institutions need to embrace and utilise this type of music in their daily activities and programmes. Principals and other key leaders should consider reviewing and revising the curriculum to include creative ideas in presenting the components of the Bible. This will help to develop and widen the knowledge of the students in their presentations of any particular subject area.

God requires His standards to be exhibited in the lives of our children and youths so that nations can be transformed for His glory. Gospel reggae, because it is scripturally based, is the prescription that will eradicate crime and violence; stop derogation of women; prevent suicide and suicidal thoughts and tendencies, sexual and physical abuse, promiscuous behaviours and poverty. For the success, longevity and continued impact of this music, the artiste has to stay connected to the true source, God Himself, to maintain the originality and radical delivery.

Reggae Dance

With this thrust in this music, God has creatively involved the dance to add another evangelical dimension. It is from this background that the dance is created either spontaneously or choreographically to be demonstrated with energy, dynamism and focus, to bring change.

Early in this chapter, mention was made of the different characteristics in reggae music; Accents, Tones, Rhythms, Energy.

Accents

Accents in reggae music tend to have a stronger emphasis on the notes when played or sung. So, in the choreographic elements, different parts of the body – hands, feet, shoulders, hips – are able to move either together or against each other using contrasting movements.

Tones

Tones are like shades in gospel reggae music. Within the different tones you are able to detect warfare, worship, praise and different forms of emotion. Jeremiah 1:10 speaks about uprooting, tearing down and building up. In the dance, the hands are dismantling strongholds and uprooting demonic forces of darkness (warfare). The feet show subjugation of the enemy. In Joshua 10:24, Joshua ordered the men to put their feet on the necks of the five kings to subdue them, which shows that God's people should have dominion over the enemy.

Rhythm

Rhythm is an indispensable element in all music. There is a distinct rhythm that comes in gospel reggae music that is dominant, flavourful and bouncy, which keeps you going. These dynamic qualities enable the choreographer to structure a sequence quickly and they also allow the dancer to dance with an abandonment.

Energy

Based on the three characteristics above, the energy in gospel reggae music is automatic. Based on this energy, coupled with the Holy Spirit, the flow of movements becomes easier. Breakthroughs happen almost immediately for those who are depressed, lost, rejected and suicidal.

So, the original concept that God intended for music and dance is to overcome the negative influences we've experienced so that restoration of lives can be achieved. This type of music is God-given and everlasting. He created the dance to give a more visible impact. Music, coupled with the dance, sets the stage for hope and deliverance.

True Revelation of God's Heart

This move of God is so dynamic and diverse that it brought a rippling effect that has changed and is still changing mindsets and destroying strongholds. God began to reveal Himself to Lester Lewis, Change, Carlene Davis, Papa San, Lieutenant Stitchie, Prodigal Son, Moses, Chevelle Franklin and recently other new gospel artistes to accent that change. Danny Browne, a transformed arranger of music, was now on the horizon and gospel reggae music was now emerging, projecting warning to the enemy's camp. There was a redeemed culture of Christian artistes and dancers who were on a mission to disturb, recapture and integrate this new move of God.

Our experiences of this diverse change started when God introduced gospel reggae music to Praise Academy of Dance at its inception in 1995. Hence began our local ministry, which was extended internationally to Bahamas,

Barbados, USA, South Africa, Australia, Trinidad, England, Puerto Rico, Canada, Curacao and Grand Cayman.

We were overcome by the overwhelming responses from the different audiences in terms of persons receiving salvation. Others experienced healing, deliverance and freedom to use this new expression in their churches and as an evangelical tool.

Many of our churches in Jamaica and the wider Caribbean are now embracing reggae music and dance, not just for entertainment, but for definite ministry.

Chapter 2

God's Purpose for Music

Psalm 19:1

"The heavens declare the glory of God;

And the firmament shows His handiwork."

Music plays a very intricate role in everyone's growth and development from birth to adulthood. Many of us grew up in different environments and cultures with numerous musical sounds around us with epic moments of joy, sadness and sometimes pain. Some of us were the creators of various sounds and instruments because that's how we were created, in the image and likeness of God, so we are His reflections on Earth.

Many persons do not know that the Bible contains many scriptures about music. Some are based on different emotions of praise, worship, warfare, fear, pain and laughter. When God created music, His purpose was very specific and that meant it was special to Him and was properly defined.

As mentioned in the Introduction, whatever God made perfect was usurped by Satan and so He has to redeem and restore everything for His glory.

Colossians 1:16 states:

"For in him all things were created: things in heaven and on earth, visible and invisible, whether thrones or powers or rulers or authorities; all things have been created through him and for him."

As I researched both Old and New Testament, I observed that different characters experienced moments of crisis, joy, pain, laughter and happiness. These experiences were varied and are identifiable with some of our situations today. Music was the therapy used to alleviate the emotions and bring back that peace and comfort to their situation.

Dedication of Solomon's Temple

In 2 Chronicles 5, the Ark of the Covenant was requested by Solomon to be one of the highlights at the dedication of Solomon's Temple, with sacrifices and playing of music. A rich blend of voices and instruments in praise and worship troubled God's nostrils.

An immediate response from God was inevitable and tangible—a cloud filled the temple, signifying the presence of the Holy God. The atmosphere was charged. It was a clear sound of melodious worship glorifying the author of music. The response caused the heart of Solomon to rejoice because God's approval was what he desired.

The Psalms

It's so interesting to know that music is evident in almost every chapter of the Psalms. So many transcripts, hymns, choruses and various compositions of music have come from these psalms. The messages of trust, hope, encouragement, forgiveness, healing and salvation have permeated the earth from these pages, showing the significance of music.

Other Purposes Established for Music

Music was used to teach and illustrate as well as communicate with God directly, bringing specific joy and peace to troubled lives and situations. A clear example of this was King Saul, who was troubled by an evil spirit and needed help.

1 Samuel 16:23, says:

"And it came to pass, when the evil spirit came upon Saul, that David took an harp and played with his hands so Saul was refreshed and was healed and the evil spirit departed from him."

Music is thought to be therapeutic and today many persons have experienced and accepted this to be accurate and evident.

All music is from God but not all music glorifies Him. His desire is to reclaim this well thought-out part of His creation for His redemptive purpose. Reggae is from the Heart of God and is integral and relevant in this time. If you reflect on the acronym in Chapter 1 you would remember that '**R**' says *Redeemed from the hands of the enemy*, the first '**G**' says *God Given*, and the last '**E**' says it's *Everlasting*.

As the Lord shared His heart with me about reggae, I came to realise more and more that this genre has a spiritual download to tear down and dismantle strongholds, as well as to build lasting and impactful structures in lives of people, communities and nations.

Reggae is not an ordinary type of music. It's a deep sound coupled with the Word of God to bring salvation, healing and deliverance. Its purpose is to bring effective change to the moral fabric of nations by eliminating the negatives and installing the positives.

Chapter 3

The Effects of Reggae Music

In this chapter, I explain the effects of reggae music on the mind, which affects the home, the community and the nation.

Romans 12:1-2 states:

> *"I beseech you therefore brethren, by the mercies of God, that you present your bodies a living sacrifice, holy, acceptable unto God which is your reasonable service. And do not be conformed to this world, but be transformed by the renewing of your mind, that you may prove what is that good and acceptable and perfect will of God."*

I am a dance teacher who was converted from a secular dancer to a Christian dancer to deliver the gospel message of Jesus Christ through dance. Therefore I'm able to attest to the effects that music has on the mind, both negative and positive in our homes, communities and our nation.

The Mind

The Oxford and Webster dictionaries describe the mind as:

1. The element of a person that enables them to be aware of the world and their experiences, to think, and to feel; the faculty of their consciousness and thought

2. a person's ability to think and reason, the intellect

Other definitions of the mind:

1. Intention; purpose; design

2. Inclination; will; desire

3. Opinion; as to express one's mind

4. Memory; remembrance

5. The intellect or intelligent power in man, considered to be centre of our emotions

So considering the different definitions mentioned, we can all agree that the mind is designed as the central part of the brain to be aware; be able to think and reason; have desires, emotional capacity and memory skills. Therefore, the mind is the control centre of our lives for everything for the whole man.

2 Timothy 1:7 says:

"God has not given us a spirit of fear, but of power and of love and of a SOUND mind." [emphasis mine]

The mind is designed to operate in a Christ-like manner, with moral values and concepts displaying an overall attitude of Christ. However, that's the place where the enemy distracts us to blur our focus.

In the earlier chapters, different reasons were given as to why music is such a powerful force as one of the art forms responsible for transformation of the human mind, either for better or worse. So the mind has the option to accept what edifies or reject what doesn't contribute to the moral fabric of our lives as it relates to music, along with everything else. Since music was inspirationally created by God for His purpose and for His glory, worship and praise need to return to their original intent and purpose.

Reggae Music whether secular or gospel, as mentioned before, has a unique sound and influence.

It possesses a powerful effect on person, home, community and nations, more than any other type of music. The rhythm, sound and lyrics are very magnetic, which pulls you into a kind of euphoria, whether it is gospel or secular. Therefore the lyrics displayed should be pure, clean and innovative to bring transformation. God desires music that will change negative thinking and behaviour to positive directions and aspirations.

Positive and Negative Effects of Reggae & Dancehall

Living in Jamaica, my nation, I can identify the negative influences that music has on the minds of our children, youths and adults mainly because of what the lyrics imply. Violence and crime, hate, abuse in all forms, emotional behaviours, murder, sexual tendencies are just a few of the negatives derived from some secular music, especially coming from dancehall.

Don't get me wrong—some secular artistes have some great songs with clean lyrics, but most persons are drawn to the music that promotes the use of the gun and immoral practices.

Our artistes therefore should be held accountable for what they put out there. Also, producers should take a definite stand not to produce music with derogatory lyrics because they know the damage that the music has created and is creating.

Music is infectious on the whole man because it begins in the mind, and then it takes control of the person. So if the person focuses on lyrical content suggesting abuse and immoral concepts consistently, it will affect the personality, behavioural patterns and academic performances.

Over these years as a teacher I've had to deal with incidents of various teens who listen to raw secular dancehall music daily, with lyrics promoting demonic content. Two or more ended up having to go through several deliverance sessions, and one was eventually admitted to Ward 13 of the University Hospital of the West Indies, Jamaica. The lyrics talk about (in patois) "cut uself", "kill a bwoy", pull the trigger and many others. Others talk about badness, madness and these are destructive to the minds of the young. This content allows their imagination to become warped and wild because they assume that it's the correct response.

Vulgarity is displayed in our music videos and attire, especially in our women, promoting acceptance of it as culture. Such ludicrous visuals are disgusting to many who are trying to raise their children with wholesome values. It is with this kind of urgency that reggae music is being redeemed and God is saving more artistes so that the influence can be reversed to bring about a dramatic, effective and transformative impact.

It's now our responsibility as Christians and Christian artistes to be more constructive and strategic in our prayers to bring that rapid and lasting change to create an environment where God will inhabit our lives, in every home, community and nation.

One of the scriptures that grabbed my attention was Joshua Chapter 10:24. It was when the five kings of the Amorites came up to make war with Joshua. The Lord discomfited the enemies and the five kings fled to a cave called Makkedah.

Verse 24, says:

> *"And it came to pass when they brought out those kings unto Joshua, that Joshua called for all the men of Israel, and said unto the captains of the men of war which went with him, Come near, and put your feet upon the necks of these kings. And they came near, and put their feet upon the necks of them."*

Putting the feet on the necks, trampling, kicking, stepping on and over speak about placing the enemy under our feet. This is a position in which the enemy is being subjected, bound and powerless.

Luke 10:19 says:

> *"Behold, I give unto you power to tread upon serpents and scorpions, and over all the power of the enemy and nothing shall by any means hurt you."*

God has already released His Dunamis power in us through His Word: Papa San's song says 'step on the enemy' because our feet have already been anointed to do so.

Psalm 144:1, says:

"Blessed be the Lord, my Rock, who trains my hands for war, and my fingers for battle."

Through this music and dance, the hands will tear down, throw down, tear apart every demonic force of darkness that seeks to stop us as believers from delivering the gospel of Jesus Christ. This music has the power to shift and detect things in the atmosphere and to expose every hidden agenda of the enemy and his cohorts, many times before they carry out their attacks.

Since the inception of gospel reggae music, more persons look forward to attending concerts where these artistes are down to perform. So there's no gospel concert without a gospel reggae artiste. If there's such an event there would definitely be a loss financially.

When artistes like Papa San and DJ Nicholas who reside abroad perform, it's always a sold-out show for the promoter of the event because patrons don't see them often. Tickets for these shows can be expensive but true lovers of this music count it a joy and a privilege to be able to hear and appreciate the word of God in this fashion.

Right now many things are changing since the coronavirus invaded our lives, homes, communities, churches and nations. For many people, thoughts on life are now different. Their perspectives are changing in what inspires and interests them more, moral values have taken a new direction and many others have decided to allow the lordship of Jesus Christ to be their focal point. So I believe that a change is resonating in the lyrical content of reggae music, and it is going to be more purpose-driven and Christ-centred. I implore present artistes to set the stage for this new realignment in the gospel reggae/dancehall and secular dancehall music to enhance this type of music.

Since hatred of the colour of our skin is a root problem and has become a cancer in more of our black race, I am declaring that the gospel and secular reggae music will contribute to much of the drastic change approaching.

We'll also see a change in our inner-city communities because our children and youths will be channeling their creative juices into a more vertical connection with God, thus producing songs that will help to dismantle strongholds of oppression and bring liberation to the minds and break mindsets.

There will be fewer negative operations in crime and violence, poverty, illiteracy, sexual and immoral behaviour patterns. Academic achievements will be heightened, children and youths will see more value in themselves, community barriers will be broken, and the spiritual fabric of our nation will become stable.

The cash flow will be so overwhelmingly lucrative that our economy will blow our minds as a nation. This is where our schools, tertiary institutions and communities will become more equipped and advanced to produce on a global stage.

So as we become more aware of the kind of music God desires, we'll be awed to see how He dots the 'i's and crosses the 't's without the hitches and the blockades.

Get ready for a life-changing experience in the music of God's heart.

Chapter 4

God's Purpose for Dance

At the core of God's heart are the Arts, which He established in Heaven so that creation would be able to praise Him in all facets. Dance, like music, was established among God's people to celebrate God Himself, to acknowledge His deity, celebrate His goodness and His mercy.

Dance was pictured as a time of nightcap for Israel as they celebrated their freedom from Egypt, The Crossing of the Red Sea, Crossing of the Jordan and the Return of the Ark. For them these accomplishments were not considered lightly, based on their experiences with the Canaanites, Hittites, Perizzites and all other enemy territories.

Because of their enslavement and the hatred meted out to them throughout their journey, dance became an outlet to express their emotional experiences. 2 Samuel 6 clearly expresses David's jubilation as he danced before the Lord at the return of the Ark to Jerusalem. The spontaneity demonstrated by David shows his love for the One who created him and so He became clamorously foolish as he danced before the Lord.

Do Not Despise What You Don't Understand

Many persons do not understand relationships especially as it relates to our relationship with our Father, God. David had a bosom relationship with God, being the little shepherd boy upon the hillside with the sheep, the young man who played skillfully on the harp to relieve Saul from a menacing spirit. So this was not new—it was a climax for him.

2 Samuel 6:16:

But Michal, David's wife, "looked through a window, and saw King David leaping and dancing before the Lord; and she despised him in her heart."

Verse 20:

"And Michal the daughter of Saul came out to meet David, and said, 'How glorious was the king of Israel today, uncovering himself today in the eyes of the maids of his servants, as one of the base fellows shamelessly uncovers himself!' "

David's response: "It was before the Lord."

Punishment given (verse 23):

"Therefore Michal the daughter of Saul had no children to the day of her death."

This dance from David was a pure one from His heart that touched God's heart and God was pleased. This shows how precious dance is to the core of God's heart once it is delivered out of an anointed vessel. God's purpose for dance has not changed, so more and more He is redeeming what He established in the beginning to its original position to declare the gospel message of Jesus Christ.

Reggae gospel dance is new to many persons who either try to ignore its power or thrust it aside as worldly. My experience with this type of dance is that God needed His Word to be demonstrated visually to disarm and destroy the powers of darkness. Gospel reggae dance speaks of entering in to possess the land and take territories, dominate and extinguish the fiery darts of the enemy. It carries an electrifying element of warfare which penetrates the darkness and brings light, setting the captives free from addictions, low self-esteem, rejection and immoral practices. This type of dance cannot be executed properly unless the participants are carriers of the presence of God, because the signs and wonders must follow.

Chapter 5

Surviving Against All Odds

Contributed by Patrick Kitson, Founder, songwriter & leader of CHANGE

Did you know there is a war between Gospel and Secular (Pop) Music, which has been going on for many decades in Jamaica? Yes, right here in Jamaica where Reggae Music was born. Many of the Churches have refused to accept Gospel Reggae.

I am child who was born, bred and grown in the Pentecostal, 'Clap Hand,' Noise Making' Church of God. I have been singing in church while standing on a chair from the age of four until I needed the chair no more. My dad, though a tailor was also the pastor.

It seemed that my musical journey had started from age four, and the passion remained until this day. My dad's tailor shop, Sweet Fit Tailoring was located at 137 Orange Street, just above BEVERLY'S RECORDS. So from an early age, maybe age five I was drawn to that record shop and ice cream parlour. Pastor Eric Kitson never told me to stop going, nor did he punish me for going. I was in love with the music I was hearing, and the art works I was seeing on those LP jackets, and the seeds were being planted. The love for the Jamaican Ska music, into Rock Steady and Reggae Music, had grown and mellowed into one of my greatest passions. Let it be known that I love and appreciate all forms of music. Let it be known too, that Reggae Music for me, no, there is absolutely no competition.

The Festival Song Competition was a special time of year for me too, and of course too, there was always Fasting Service at my Dad's Church on Independence Day. I would excuse myself from The Fasting Service to go and follow the Music Truck featuring the festival songs. I would walk beside the music truck from Bumper Hall (STATHS) where it all started, to the Kingston Public Hospital (KPH), turn and walk back to Church which was off Waltham Park Road.

The year was 1972 when I was asked by the talented Dennis Haynes - Leader of INSIGHTS GOSPEL GROUP to join the group as a rhythm guitarist. At the time I was fourteen years old and playing the rhythm guitar in his dad's church. I was shocked and could not believe my ears, but he assured me that it was all real and that he liked how I played. What a day that was for me. Of course my dad did not approve, and I was eventually read out of the church. INSIGHTS had great musicians such as the Lennox Gordon (lead guitar), Tony Hutton (bass guitar), Andel Forgie (drums), and Segree Morris (rhythm guitar). There was no keyboardist, but there were numerous singers including George Banton, Dr.

Blossom White, and Trios just to name a few. My new musical journey had started. Wow! and what a journey it had been.

Many folks said that INSIGHTS was ahead of its time, and I wholeheartedly agree. INSIGHTS played to numerous congregations with mixed responses. An instrumental reggae version of a traditional chorus "The Holy Ghost Power" was one of the first Reggae songs that was performed to great responses. As an Ardenne High School Student in 1975 another traditional chorus 'Highway To Heaven' came on the scene and it hit the ground running. It was an instant crowd favourite. 'Highway To Heaven' was introduced to a tent crusade meeting of Garvey Meade in Portmore. The Pastor was Rev. Delford Davis. That song became an instant hit wherever it was performed. 'Highway' was first the reggae gospel song with a DJ section in it. As the years went on a few more reggae songs were introduced until we were invited to perform at a Seventh Day Adventist Church outside of Mandeville. It was a great afternoon, and the show was coming to a close when we performed “Highway To Heaven' and started the DJ section. The Pastor took the microphone and said, “we are turning the church into a dance hall.” That utterance hit me hard.. I saw a deacon dusting off his shoes. The church wanted to feed us after all that. I insisted for us not to partake of the food, since they didn't accept our music. This is now the fun part, our transportation back to Kingston came at about 2:30am, some band members got hungry, couldn't resist, and surrendered to their hunger, and ate the food. I stood my ground and refused. George Banton who was visiting from Canada was also on the Show. INSIGHTS were the leaders in Gospel Reggae despite the opposition from the religious crowd, and we held our ground.

The year was now 1985 when the group of young enthusiastic reggae loving musicians exited INSIGHTS and the CHANGE happened. Rehearsals started and they were glorious. The founding members were me as band leader, guitarist, vocalist, Rohan Reid (bass guitar, vocals), Mark James and Fender Rhodes (vocals), Lloyd Geddes (drums), Henry Morrison (vocals, percussion), and Merle Gayle (lead vocals). CHANGE's first performance was on its way at the Hard Court at U.W.I Mona, Campus one Friday afternoon. The audience was made of INSIGHTS faithful supporters and the curious ones wanting to hear what this new band would do. They were not disappointed as the female lead singer Merle Gayle - former Lead Singer of the Grace Thrillers, delivered beautifully. I was very surprised but totally satisfied.

I recently received a call from a friend in New York, and as he was reflecting about that same concert, I felt blessed all over again. CHANGE was on its way and we were convinced that the Father gave us the thumbs up. The news was out that the NEW SIGHTS was in town. The welcoming we were expecting from the more established gospel groups wasn't happening at all. And oh yes, I was very disappointed, but not discouraged. I realised then, that we had to start with a small circle of supporters and let it grow. That was exactly what had happened. Shortly after, migration hit the group and we had to re-group with, a new lead singer - Tony Barnes, keyboardist - John Sharpe, and drummer - Robert Stewart.

CHANGE Despite...

Controversial

Hard-Core,

Aggressive,

No-nonsense,

Gospel

Expression

On Wednesday November 15, 1995, a simple headline in The Barbados Advocate – WHAT A CHANGE – announced the band called CHANGE to Barbados. This was very encouraging for us, as this was our first trip outside of our homeland, Jamaica, the Reggae Land. CHANGE featured new members Othniel Lewis (keyboards), Michael Kennedy (bass guitar), and Yiska (Saxophone and vocals). This move facilitated the movements of founding member Rohan Reid (bass guitar and vocals) as well as Noel Wallace (keyboards). Tony Barnes, the lead singer too, had also migrated. He was replaced by the less energetic, but with a huge voice, Andrew Lawrence. The Bajan audience were on their feet from the get-go until the last note. What stood out for me then was that we didn't have any music out. Barbados was indeed a wonderful experience for CHANGE.

CHANGE has cleared the path for artistes, such as Junior Tucker, Papa San, Stitchie, Judy Mowatt, Chevelle Franklin and others in their conversion to Gospel Reggae. Incidentally, I had collaborated with Junior Tucker (now a pastor) when he became a Christian on his first gospel hit – Healing Me.

Our first self-titled 12-track CD was recorded at Grove Studios in Ocho Rios, the parent company of IRIE-FM Radio Station, and was produced by the multi-talented Stephen Stewart. A distribution deal was also penned with Freedom Records in the USA, whose parent company was Malaco Records, the largest black gospel recording label. This was a small deal with a one CD contract, and soon we were compared to groups like Boyz 2 Men and Take 6 for our artistry and harmonic tightness.

By this time CHANGE's small circle of supporters had grown immensely. The CD was launched at Stephanie Hall in 1996 to an almost sold-out crowd. The single "Take the Lord in Your Life" played on IRIE-FM's midday program for about a year, and was the closing song for Gary G's Afternoon Show. Despite all the negatives from our religious folks, CHANGE never lost sight of the mission and command to, "go into all the world and preach the Gospel." We did just that at STING at the National Stadium, REGGAE SUNSPLASH at Jam World,

Portmore, Club 24K in Manor Park, and the one that generated months of preaching and group discussions on the air waves and in the print media, was IRIE-FM's REGGAE BASH at White River Reggae Park. We were never shaken at all.

Another big one for CHANGE was when Kirk Franklin first visited Jamaica courtesy of Life Productions, and brought out the largest crowd at Cinema 2 in New Kingston. When CHANGE appeared on the Ocho Rios leg of the concert, Kirk Franklin came on singing "One for the Father" and announced that CHANGE is the "baddest band" he had heard in a long time and that he had "heard a lot of bands."

"Global Mission with Billy Graham" came calling. CHANGE and BIRTHRIGHT were selected to represent the Caribbean. Although CHANGE was rigourously opposed by the local Church leaders, this was ignored as the Production Manager knew and heard what she wanted. The song "JESUS IS LORD" was chosen. A video was done, and a re-mix of the song was requested to bring the reggae bass line down. This song was produced by the late Barry O'Hare, and CHANGE gone international again. CHANGE was also called to perform at the National Stadium for NELSON MANDELA'S visit. Perform they did. The feedback and responses were awesome. We knew what we were called to do, and the bashings were coming left, right, and centre, but we continued in our purpose despite all the challenges.

Chapter 6

The Response of the Church

Written by Pastor Courtney Morrison,
Senior Pastor, Fellowship Tabernacle Church, Portmore

Reggae and Gospel: two words which by our own culture and association would not seem to have anything one to do with the other, as diametrically opposed and as far as the East would seem from the West. Let's delve a little into our Jamaican history and culture and dissect this anatomy of our religious belief and traditions.

My journey begins from September 12, 1988, that infamous day when a hurricane of disastrous proportions ravaged the wonderful island of Jamaica in the West Indies; a time of darkness (no electricity) and stagnation (no running water) for the majority of the population of this the "Land of Wood and Water." Hurricane Gilbert had caused severe dislocation of families and the functionality of businesses and the education system of Jamaica.

Yet in all this wake of devastation and catastrophe, there were songs of hope blaring over radio stations and at every opportunity given, the levels of encouragement of starting over and rebuilding the nation were echoed from Negril Point to Morant Point, all along the breadth, length and depth of Jamaica.

In the background of all this seeming rubble, arising from the debris of all this frustration, there was a rumbling beneath the surface. Like a phoenix awakening to glory, a music form was about to arise. It would cause the youth of the church and the general body of Christ to take a serious look at how we praise and worship in Jamaica, the Caribbean and all around the world, to stand up and recognize the power of the rhythm and beat of the drums and the powerful baseline of the guitar accompanied by a slow one drop beat, to take the Gospel Fraternity by storm.

In October 1988, the Jamaica Youth For Christ was to have held their National Convention and Talents For Christ program, but it had to be cancelled in light of the majority of the island still not having their normal electricity supply and not all communities even being fully accessible by roads. A great visionary and my mentor, Mr. Andrew Stone, had commissioned having the convention to become a time of prayer and so the igniting of a new era was about to be fanned into an inferno.

Genesis, a gospel concert (a vision given to Andrew Stone), held immediately following Watch Night (New Year's Eve) Service January 1, 1989, was about to explode in even literal ways that could not have been foretold or even seemingly prophesied.

It was on a cool morning of January 1, 1989. A young man, a great friend and his team took to the stage in the 4 am of that dark morn. He belted out a very popular church song – "I must hold to His hands, God's unchanging hands." The congregation rose in thunderous applause and delightful singing until the song took a twist. No one expected what would happen next. He changed the rhythm to solid hardcore reggae and the remix of the song silenced the overwhelmingly Pentecostal-based audience.

Silence reigned. In Jamaica we would declare, "Angel ah pass through." It would seem that the very Angels would become bystanders to human behaviour. Some of the attendees in voicing their displeasure of the remix with Reggae, a defilement of the sacred song, pelted the lead Gospel artiste and his accompanist with missiles of various sorts. This event made the headlines of the national newspaper the following day. This was the beginning of the first visible assault launched against Gospel Reggae.

In the meantime another storm of pandemic proportions was brewing in a most prestigious organisation of Youth(s) for Christ. A set of twins, Karl Downer and Caren Downer (Morrison), became energized and compelled in their beliefs that most of the secular reggae songs could become transformed by simply changing the lyrics of these songs and Christianized (Gospelized), thereby baptizing them and making them fit for the Christian fraternity. Karl and Caren would take every opportunity to present their Reggae Gospel duo everywhere they went. These two, along with Junior Miller, Adrian Smith, Horace and Peter McDonald were the unsung heroes of the beginning of the rise of Gospel Reggae.

The Nelson Mandela Park, Skateland (Half-Way-Tree) and Kingston Youth For Christ were some of the platforms graced with their presentation of the revolutionary new sounds in the Christian arena. There were the more popular Love Singers, the great and indomitable group named Change, Grace Thrillers, Living Stones and Cross Culture who were a major part of this exciting wind of transformation that blew across the hills, mountains and plains of the great nation of Jamaica.

The release of a new sound in the Gospel fraternity was causing discomfort and unrest among many. The Gospel group Change made an illustrious appearance on one of Reggae's largest stage show platforms, quite to the protest of many churches and Church leaders. Yet this soul-stirring band made the headlines of one of the nation's leading papers which compared them to the Steel Pulse Band, the top Reggae band internationally, even declaring that Change outshone all other bands and was on the same level as Steel Pulse. It was at this very presentation that a lead gospel artiste was saved after Andrew Lawrence (Change's lead singer) spoke with him and his conversion process began.

At The Jamaica National Arena, in Genesis 1991 at which I was prayer coordinator, there was the second upheaval as Change made their presentation in the Gospel Premium concert. A member of the band had to take the mike and vehemently sought to ask the crowd if the behaviour they were displaying was Christian. It seemed as if it was déjà vu of Genesis January 1989 as missiles were again flung on stage and at the artiste.

The way was paved for our current crop of Gospel Reggae artistes by these great revolutionary pioneers of the frontier in Gospel Reggae. The group of Katalyst Crew, led by the lion himself

Paul Barclay cannot go without mention. They helped in starting a new wave of dances in Reggae Gospel. Christian Youths would be singing and dancing and jumping, belting out *"narrow road, narrow road, follow di cross, follow di cross, whip di devil, whip di devil"* from one of the group's biggest hits. The chain reaction had begun. Similar to a nuclear bomb there arose like a mushroom cloud, blanketing the Christian community with a plethora of Gospel Reggae artistes: the CEO himself – Prodigal (formerly known as Blessed), Papa San (Tyrone Thompson), Stitchie and the Late Moses (Kasim Grant), to name a few. The church now had to come face to face with this new phenomenon.

Many others took up the mantle and made tremendous strides in presenting the art form in all its glory.

There was the emergence of DJ Nicholas, Prodigy (Pastor Ryan Mark) and Jason Mighty to name a few others.

Gospel concerts across the nation had a new face, dance teams now also had to alter their styles to match the changes of this new tsunami which was now predominantly the choice of the youths in most churches.

Dance groups such as the Praise Academy of Dance, led by the anointed visionary lady Dr. Patrica Noble, were now in a position of recognising that this move of God was the direction of promise.

Chapter 7

Through the Lens of the Diaspora

Written by

Patricia Cox – Founding Member of Praise Academy of Dance, Barbados

Angela B. Slack – Founding Member of Praise Academy of Dance, Jamaica

Patricia Cox

My name is Patricia Cox, aka Aunty Pat and I am from your sister island Barbados. I fell in love with Jamaica some years back—first its music, then its people, then its food.

From as far back as I can remember I had always loved dancing. Maybe it's my mother who got me started in dance.

Or maybe God saw me from a child and orchestrated my steps by using her. My mother loved dancing: Three step, Two step, The Bump, Rock the Boat. From about five years old she would put me to stand on her feet and dance with me or she would position my feet on the floor and teach me. Those were my molding years...Thank you Mummy.

Now let me fast forward to later years. I have danced at local, regional and international events, with various dance groups, as a back-up dancer for performing calypsonians and music videos. I have had my bout in the hotel circuit. I have also choreographed for a number of people and groups over the years.

As a dancer, choreographer and an island girl, I have been exposed to several genres of dance and music, but my all-time favourite is Reggae. Reggae is raw. It makes no apologies for what it is. It's a rhythm that's built inside your bones. For me it's natural – a natural movement – and your body just moves with it. Don't try to tame it or you will miss the message in the lyrics and the beauty in the dance. That's because reggae music and its lyrics are life. It talks about love and hurt, kindness and hatred, hard times and good times, respect for yourself and your fellow man. It can be warm or harsh like life is at times. Whatever it is, it brings a community and people together.

Reggae is bold. It's as bold as my Jamaican family. Needless to say when I hear reggae it awakens boldness in me. It's "Watch me now, this is my time."

So when I became a Christian I knew I still wanted to dance. People wanted to tame me. What I was accustomed to wasn't acceptable in the church. So you can imagine me with my locs down my back as a Christian just wanting to "bust out" and dance. I had no formal training, just a raw passion to dance.

That's when I started dancing with a group we dubbed "The Gospelfest Dancers." Gospelfest is an annual event. It attracts gospel artistes from the Caribbean and across the globe. Local dance groups are also invited to participate. It was during that time that Jamaican Ms. Cynthia Patrica Noble, also known as Aunty Pat to us, Founder and the then Director of Praise Academy of Dance Jamaica, came to Barbados. She taught us the dances for Gospelfest and then left me to oversee and change the dances as I saw fit and get them ready for the stage. That was the beginning of a new chapter for me as a choreographer.

Eventually Praise Academy of Dance was started in Barbados by Cynthia Patrica Noble, with Marcia Weekes, also a Jamaican born, as the Artistic Director. I became one of the founding members. As the years went by, Praise Academy of Dance Barbados grew in size and became known for excellence and, like our Motto says, "Changing mindsets Through Creative Expression," that's just what we did.

We choreographed and danced to many genres of dance but when Praise Academy of Dance Barbados first started to venture into Reggae, It was Praise Academy of Dance Jamaica who came here and taught us their dance to Papa San's "Pop Style". When we came to the stage with this dance the young people were screaming. Everyone knew Papa San and Pop Style. Everyone knows Jamaica and Reggae. So here comes Barbados to join Jamaica and people couldn't wait to see the amalgamation. They weren't disappointed.

These two cultures gave a top of the chain performance: passion, energy, attitude, synergy. All these attributes signify life and that is what Reggae is all about.

Through the years Praise Academy of Dance Barbados became very popular and more children started to attend. I was approached by The Artistic Director Mrs. Marcia Weekes about becoming a ministry leader for the very young girls from about ages six to ten years. Well after much prayer, I got my release to accept the offer.

From here on it was just excitement. God saw fit to put me over this group of very young ladies to mentor, teach and mold. They didn't just learn choreography, they learned about life. They learned principles and discipline. They were encouraged to do things like packing their own bags for classes or rehearsals and preparing their snacks.

The dance group was called Promise, but the name was changed to Children of Promise. These children were energetic and ready to dance. God gave me the strength, wisdom and vision to be the ministry leader He asked me to be. This junior group became well known for their energetic and well executed dances. They broke the barriers with their unconventional moves that the church would not even dare attempt. After all, most church dance ministries were only into the slow liturgical choreography where only hands were used or flags or streamers most of the time. Reggae was different. My style was different. I was different. So, we broke the mold.

Yes we were frowned upon by some "church folk," especially the older people who thought reggae didn't belong in the church or it wasn't godly. It took some getting used to for them and still some haven't come to terms with it as yet. Reggae involves the entire body, not just hands and a spin. Now the dance moves weren't what I would have done before I was a Christian –definitely not – but they certainly weren't timid and tamed either. Reggae movements are exaggerated, large. Some say it is larger than life. They exemplify the music, the lyrics and its message.

It wasn't the Church who first respected or accepted us—it was the secular world. They saw excellence and professionalism and that's what they wanted. We took God with us wherever we went and preached the word through our dance.

Children of Promise went on and were involved in many local competitions. The two major competitions in Barbados were National Independence Festival of Creative Arts (NIFCA) and The Community Dance Fest. Almost all dance groups participated in these. No one cared if you were the Church. The same rules applied to all and the same privileges. Yes we added a different element with our reggae compared to the secular groups, but our dances were clean, well executed, energetic and always told a story. That's why every year Children of Promise would medal at NIFCA and come in the top three at The Community Dance Fest competitions.

As I mentioned before, I used all genres, but whenever we danced to reggae people paid extra attention. Even these young dancers, whenever reggae music was played, were eager to dance and try the moves and bring their own. Reggae is about everyday life so you can take just about any move and tell a story. Something as simple as a walk, you can add your own attitude, body language and style and dance it like you own it.

My young dancers were all so little when they started, and it has blessed my heart to see that they are all grown up.

Most of them still dance. Some have gone off to study overseas or pursue a dance career. I remember at a dance exam one young dancer thanked me for all the time I had invested in her. There was a dance style she couldn't get done, but thanks to the ministry team Children of Promise, and exposure to the various dance genres we did, she was able to finally nail it for her dance exam group piece. What makes me laugh is when they were in choreography with other dancers someone would say, "Wait, Aunty Pat taught you?"

My greatest joy is to see these young ladies on stage dancing with me. If I call on them now to dance a reggae piece they still remember like they did it just yesterday. That gives me a great feeling. Then I know I have impacted their lives positively.

Yes I'm older but trust me I can still "buss" a reggae dance anytime. As a matter of fact I tell my friends; in Heaven I'm going to be leading the reggae section. Yea, watch me now.

Angela B. Slack

As a trainee teacher, I had found that there had been a natural resistance to academic subjects by many kinesthetic or visual learners. I struggled to engage these learners. Then one day, I remembered a simple rhyme with movements that I learned in nursery school. It used hand movements, to follow along to a simple song, to teach basic numeracy skills. Why haven't I forgotten it and others like it? This question dogged me for a long time, and I was determined to find the answer.

So, for my teacher training thesis, I investigated the use of dance and drama in history teaching, and this gave me the freedom to use music and movement in the classroom. The results were great. Music and movement seem to lock in information in our long-term memory as it is recording a pleasant experience, not just banal information. Furthermore, it collapsed barriers to learning such as class, ability, economics and removed inhibitions about self-image. Later on, when I taught in UK schools, reggae music became a bridge between the two cultures, and I had wonderful results as learners connected to this music. It greatly aided my delivery of academic subjects.

There is also much to be said about the effectiveness in communication when using the heart language or the mother tongue of any people and Reggae Music uses the Jamaican patois to communicate its message. It is couched in syncopated Afro-beats that have been synthesised over the years to become what reggae is today.

I had a conversation with a colleague and ethno-musicologist recently. She stated that in a survey that she did she had responses from Jamaicans who said that when they worship using European and other foreign musical forms, there is a delay-effect. This constitutes their translation of the English words, then it enters into their spirits.

Conversely, reggae music has no such delay. I have never considered this before since the official language of Jamaica is English, but it is not the heart language of the people, and the heart always responds to its own first. Similarly, if you attend any church service, gospel meeting or concert and Reggae Gospel Music is used as a part of the praise and worship, the response from the congregation is immediately explosive. Why? I suggest that it is because Reggae is our indigenous music form, and our souls know it best and therefore respond without inhibition; it's in our DNA.

Reggae is the heart music of Jamaica and embodies its cultural evolution and when coupled with the truth of the gospel it takes on a powerfully magnetic and catalytic effect. It pulls us to God and starts a regenerative process within our hearts. We must not be shy to use it.

Chapter 8

Visible Impact

God said something was missing from His creative plan

He made man and was not satisfied

Took a rib from the man and called her woman

When God established Praise Academy

Contemporary flavour was what we had

God intervened into the puzzle

The empty void was filled because

The missing nugget was Reggae music

That He needed to complete His plan

To restore His original kingdom

Colossians chapter 1, verse 16 says

Everything was created by Him for His glory

So when we jump up and say

Mi ha mi Ting pon mi, mi ha mi Ting pon mi

Is my Bible, Bible, not a gun

We just a tek back to bring back His glory

To spread the gospel message far and wide

So wid we hands we tear down and build up

Wid de feet we trample and demolish

Snakes and scorpions cyaa hurt us

Because power and authority inna wi mouth and wi feet

Reggae music and dance you cyaa ignore

It nuh watch nuh face - it just activate

Leaving so many in awe as music and dance coordinate

Leaving you breathless as you watch

Not wanting to let this moment escape

But to let it linger as you soak yourself in

This music and dance is the visible impact

That has and will continue

To change mindsets and cultures

With ritualistic binds and bondages

Churches so set in their usual routine

Not having a vision to change

This is the moment, the season

For this visible impact to invade

The hearts of the young and not so young

So our children and teens can find hope

In a God who is not dead but alive

Carrying an aroma that causes lives

To be enraptured with the presence

Of a creative God with a great sense of humour

A music that was once taboo is now breaking

Down walls of tradition and embracing

We own diverse culture, yes reggae music is here to stay forever and ever

Grab onto it, run wid it, love it

Visible like never before wid

Deeper depths and higher heights

Inna God who is unchangeable

Unshakable and unstoppable

Written by: Dr C Patrica Noble

Chapter 9

Miracles, Signs & Wonders of Reggae Music & Dance

Mark 16:17-18 says:

"And these signs shall follow them that believe; In My name shall they cast out devils; they shall speak with new tongues; They shall take up serpents; and if they drink any deadly thing, it shall not hurt them; they shall lay hands on the sick, and they shall recover."

Praise Academy of Dance Jamaica has travelled extensively to many countries, namely South Africa, Australia, England, the United States of America, Canada, Puerto Rico, Barbados, Trinidad, Curacao and Grand Cayman. In all of our ministries in these countries we have seen and experienced signs and wonders that have left us speechless and overwhelmingly blessed to see The Holy Spirit at work. In my first book, The Journey Continues..., some of them were mentioned but in case you didn't purchase a copy I will highlight a few.

1998 - Cincinnati, Ohio, USA

Two persons along traveled with me to Cincinnati, Ohio to attend a dance workshop facilitated by Dr. Lyrica Smith. The presentation was on reggae and was attended by various representatives from different dance ministries. This was their first experience in using another genre that is not contemporary. For them there was a new discovery of an awareness of their body and that other parts of their bodies can move without vulgarity.

It was a strange encounter with the Holy Spirit at work in the minds and bodies of these dancers.

They were surprisingly overwhelmed knowing that this was a new dimension of music and dance of which they weren't aware. So it released them into realising that God can use another genre apart from the contemporary to glorify Himself.

2000 - Cincinnati, Ohio, USA

In the year 2000, Dr. Lyrica Smith hosted another Dance Conference in which I was a Reggae Workshop Presenter. Although there were various workshops, the one for reggae was the largest. However, the Holy Spirit intervened because the host advised me that the Lord wanted me to teach the three hundred (300) persons all at the same time.

This was divinely orchestrated because I received the instructions of how the class should be structured. The Lord led me to the Exodus of the Israelites from Egypt to Canaan. The warm-up session was the preparation. For the progressions across the floor, the starting point was Egypt, and the end was Canaan. On reaching Canaan they were to claim their healing and breakthroughs for any situations they were going through. The music used was "Mi Ha Mi Ting Pon Mi" (which is the Bible) by Lester Lewis.

At the end of the session I was the only one standing. There was crying, hugging, anxious faces and the sweet presence of the Lord. It was then revealed to me by the host, Dr. Lyrica Smith, that Cincinnati, Ohio had a racial barrier, and this was the first time that blacks and whites had the opportunity to be in the same space actually rubbing shoulders. Thus a spirit of healing and forgiveness was inevitable because God knows the end from the beginning. Another woman who was present after major surgery of a cyst at the back of her head found the dressing had dropped off, leaving no evidence of the cut.

Also, although 300 persons were at the workshop, only 299 participated because a white woman from UK thought the dance and music was too black for her. So there she was back in England after one week, lying prostrate on her belly, being chastised by the Lord. In her apology she remarked that God told her that because she suffered from racism, He took His daughter from Jamaica to destroy that spirit so she could be free and she ignored it.

This genre of music and dance as was mentioned before changes situations, reverses curses and submerges the undesirable negatives that always present itself among God's people.

July 1997 - South Africa Dance Conference

After the dissolution of Apartheid in South Africa, the white Christians wanted to help to evangelise black volatile communities but weren't bold enough and were very afraid of any retaliation. So our presence at this conference as Praise Academy of Dance from Jamaica presented the opportunity for them to do this outreach. The request was accepted enthusiastically because we really wanted to see people who looked like us.

We approached the market square with excitement, not knowing what to expect. As we alighted from the bus clad in our Jamaican shirts and started to set up with reggae music blaring, the vendors abandoned their wares and gathered around us. As we danced, they responded with cheerful laughter and then seeing that the presence of the Lord was so tangible, we prayed and were able to lead many to Christ. That music was Reggae, not Contemporary. That's the effect reggae has on the minds and because the atmosphere was charged with the anointing, and His presence was tangible, the signs were inevitable.

1998 & 2004 - London, England

For the first time Londoners saw a visual live performance/ministry of a type of music and dance that was new to them. They came from four directions throwing their arms, shaking their shoulders and moving their feet with an energy we never expected. You could identify the 'Yardie' because they really were pumping the movements. The air was charged, and the people were interactive and wanted more and more. Lives were ministered to because of the anointing coming from both music and dance. People weren't afraid to abandon themselves like David did because they realised that a change was coming into their lives that they had never experienced before.

2004 - Jamaica, New York, USA

Allen Cathedral Dance Conference

"Woe," one of Prodigal Son's hit songs, was done at the park in Jamaica, New York. Let's laugh a little. The day started with just some contemporary songs with dancers from different States in America mingling around with no one from the communities.

However, the DJ belched out "Woe" and I saw people running from all directions. Some were still in nightwear, shorts, setters in the hair; they heard a familiar music. Then the dancers hit the stage and it was pandemonium. The dancers had to dance twice. Reggae Gospel and dance stole the spotlight.

2006 - Outreach to Six Flags, New York, USA

Allen Cathedral Dance Conference

As part of the conference schedule there is generally an evangelistic outreach to Six Flags which we were excited about. This was an amusement facility we always heard about but really wanted to experience in real life. Now because the organisers realised that the environment we were entering into demanded our focus, prayers of warfare echoed throughout the area, preparing for the ministry of reggae music and dance.

The Jamaican reggae music started pumping with "Gimme Gimme" by Papa San, "Revival" and "Holy Ghost Church" by DJ Nicholas. Streams of people began to rush in to see what was happening. It was a mixture of laughter, joy and dynamic reggae movements with everyone participating with a sway of the hands and juggling of the feet.

2000 - Mittagong, Sydney Australia

Christian International Dance Conference

This is an interesting, eventful and indescribable mission. We arrived in Australia without our luggage after missing our targeted flight. However, we weren't flustered by the derailment because winter clothes were provided for us and interestingly all of us got the right sizes.

The Aborigines were delighted to see us, because they saw where we looked like them. Persons who attended the International Christian Dance Conference in South Africa in 1997 were anxious to see us again. Excitement filled the air on ministry night as Lieutenant Stitchie's music barked from the stage as we danced. Some were experiencing this type of music and dance for the very first time.

Workshops

Thus the reggae workshops were filled and overflowing as different persons from different countries just soaked up these reggae movements. A fresh and new sound invaded the territory and brought joy to the heart of the people. Put no limits or boundaries on God because He uses the foolish things of the world to confound the wise.

As we do outdoor ministry on the streets locally, it is interesting to note that the reggae music and dance are the most captivating and rewarding elements in our Evangelism

Explosion. Many persons of mixed ages look forward to these moments to interact and make decisions to charter a new path to life.

We simply label these experiences as treasures placed in God's treasure book of memoirs/memories.

If we as Christian dancers and musicians try to engage our youths in the inner-city communities with a more creative, godly way to utilise their talents, then there would be more positive reinforcement and discipline in our homes, communities, schools, and churches, thus a better nation under God. This is a great opportunity to use this genre of music and dance to spread the gospel message of Jesus Christ to give our children and youths a more encouraging and stable lifestyle in which to exist. The ground is fertile for this seed to be planted where it will be watered by another minister and God will bring the increase.

Chapter 10

Street Vibes

Written by Keisha Campbell Prayer Coordinator, Praise Academy of Dance, Jamaica

September 2020 - Setting the Scene

It was crescendo after crescendo as the intensity of the wind pulsated through the trees, causing branches and leaves to be immersed in this grand performance of energetic dance. It was nature in concert and oh it is beautiful. Creation ongoingly declares the glory of God and continues to testify of His greatness.

Many people around the world are too busy to even notice the beautiful performance of nature that continues to glorify God by its very existence. Many also do not attend church, listen to gospel radio stations, listen to gospel music or even watch gospel television programs. Nonetheless, they need to hear the gospel. Mark 16 vs 15 states:

"He said to them, "Go into all the world and preach the gospel to all creation."

This requires that believers of Jesus of Christ take the good news to the people in the streets. This is being done in many areas across the world and one effective way of ministering the gospel has been to use Gospel Reggae Music with dance to attract people to hear the good news. Dancing in the street is connecting with the people, demonstrating that we feel you, you are not alone, we are standing with you. We are not far off from your experiences. We will meet you in the street with what we have to offer, which is the good news of salvation through Jesus Christ.

This good news is authentic and life-changing, so utilising the energy and authenticity of dancing reggae gospel, signals that in this time and space we are standing in the gap for you, we are powerfully interceding for you with movements that trample serpents and scorpions. The energy and tenacity of dancing Gospel Reggae is a sniper attack in the enemy's camp, as the movements strike a blow to principalities and powers, rulers of darkness and wickedness in high places. On several occasions we have observed deliverance from unclean spirits just from the ministry of the dance and reggae music.

The Atmosphere

2 Corinthians 10:4-5

"For the weapons of our warfare are not carnal but mighty in God for pulling down strongholds, casting down arguments and every high thing that exalts itself against the knowledge of God, bringing every thought into captivity to the obedience of Christ."

This scripture serves as a great platform to stand on for ministry in the streets. A case in point, in many interviews across the world, an ex-Satanist has indicated that one of the nightly practices of him and many others like him was to visit different regions and curse them. Therefore, when you enter an area to conduct outdoor ministry, it is already established that there will be warfare. However, as the scripture indicates, our weapons are not carnal; they are mighty through God. So, from the very first sound of the reggae beat a tremor is sent in the atmosphere similar to that of a giant stomping his feet to signal that he is present. Gospel Reggae penetrates the atmosphere like a bullet ripping through the air. It rips through the air to shake strongholds and hit the very foundation of evil in the area. Reggae music declaring the gospel is a mighty weapon in the hand of God. Set the stage for outdoor ministry in dance or any other outdoor initiative for God by saturating the atmosphere with the influential sounds of Gospel Reggae music. Joshua sent the worshippers ahead of the army when going into battle and we can too by using Gospel Reggae music as one of the genres of gospel music played at street events. Irrespective of the fact that Satan is the Prince of the Power of the Air – Ephesians 2 vs 1-3 – God is mighty, and he has given us the Power and Authority to defeat the devil.

Attention-Grabbing

Ministry in the streets connotes that “wi ago tek it to dem” meaning we are taking the gospel message to their doorsteps. This objective requires laser sharp focus and using a methodology that is highly effective with great impact. Take a journey with me to a busy city market on a weekend. There is much activity in a city market, similar to that of a disturbed ant's nest where the ants are frantically running to and fro. In the midst of this busyness, merchants are feverishly competing for the attention of shoppers. To accomplish this, over the last decade it became increasingly popular to play music at its loudest decibel to attract customers to their location and it worked. The music is usually energetic and "full of vibes," coupled with a gentleman on a microphone calling out the deals being offered by the merchant.

Ministering in these streets means competing with the merchants' loud music to get the attention of the people. Is that even possible you may think? Yes, it is possible. With prayer as a foundation, just set up the music system at a strategic location and begin to play the Gospel Reggae and make room for the dancers. The power and the force coming from the Gospel Reggae beat with words of power and might, collaborating with the authority of the stomping of the feet, the power in the hands and shoulders, partnered with the nodding of the head all become magnetised and begin to lure people to the area just to see what is going on. There it is, you have grabbed their attention and now that you have it, maximize it. It is time to use ingenuity and share the gospel with onlookers.

Using ingenuity to share the gospel increases the effectiveness of evangelism and there are multiple ways to increase the effectiveness of outdoor evangelism. Let us explore this.

The aroma of heat activating herbs and spices dances the waltz with the gentle wind that is sweeping through the narrow streets of this inner-city community. It is a Sunday afternoon, and the homes are saturated with home-cooked meals where the wonderful aromas have danced out of the homes into the streets providing an exquisite experience for the nostrils. This is the norm on a Sunday afternoon, along with the setting up of the sound system at the biggest shop in the area. The occasional testing of the speakers indicates to the community that they will soon be feted with the usual myriad of songs from all genres, starting with Gospel that is not usually featured for an extended period. This is the culture of the people.

However, this is an ideal setting for street ministry. Sunday evening service could occasionally take the form of street ministry of not just handing out tracks to households but coordinating a Gospel Reggae Dance session to win their attention and sow the seed of the good news. This is strategically utilising the culture to minister the gospel.

Community members are acclimatized to hearing loud secular music blaring from sound systems being played in the community, so setting up something similar with a playlist of only Gospel Reggae will stimulate interest. This then becomes the pulling factor for them to experience the ministry in dance. The pulsating swing of every shoulder and hand, along with the dominating authoritative stomp of the feet shod with the preparation of peace after dismantling the strongholds in the lives of onlookers, will create a ripple impact in their lives as people have experienced deliverance in these moments. In adapting to their environment of loud music and dancing by playing loud Gospel Reggae music in conjunction with dance to minister the Gospel, we demonstrate that we understand you and your lifestyle and Jesus wants to meet you right where you are—right there in the inner-city.

Dance is dynamic and so is reggae music. These two powerful tools united for the Kingdom of God are effective mechanisms for spreading the good news. They are formidable weapons in the hands of God as we allow the Holy Spirit to use us in the Earth to be his witnesses. Let us throw aside all limitations as to what God can do and what He can use to do it. Let us submit to the leading of the Holy Spirit to fulfil the will of God and influence the atmosphere, grab people's attention and connect with them for the purpose of winning souls and setting the captives free.

Chapter 11

Tek It To Dem

What a day, a moment, a time, and a season when reggae music and dance erupted on the contemporary scene of things! Different changes emerged that even we as leaders couldn't comprehend. But as I said before, God had a sense of humour when He created Reggae Music.

Emotions, body language, behaviour patterns, attitudes, responses, stage presence and a sense of belonging facilitated a more expressive acceptance of our own culture. No fear, no scorn—just a peace as the vibes of music and dance dominated the hearts and captured the minds of those who waited for such an incredible sound and movements that related to their situations.

This chapter "Tek It To Dem" echoes the above changes that were brought about when reggae music and dance disrupted our ministry in a positive way.

The day has finally come when Gospel Reggae Music and Dance rise to the top of the chart. What a welcoming overture to a new era that will enable our children and youths to find new outlets to develop their gifts and talents in a holistic way.

Photos from Praise Academy of Dance, Jamaica & Barbados

hotography

12:32
PRAISE ACADEMY OF DANCE
PRESENTS THE
ULTIMATE GOSPEL REGGAE DANCE CONCERT
REGGAE
VIBEZ
"FREE D.A.T.A"
FEATURING DANCE MINISTERS:
Laud Dance Ministry
EBF Dance Troupe
FellTab Dance Ministry (Portmore)
Portmore Missionary Dance Ministry
V.O.W Dance Ministry
and hosts:
Praise Academy of Dance
Guest Artiste
JPROJEK
Guest Artiste
CHRISANDO
CHRISTIE
March 5, 2016
Covenant City Church
72 Half Way Tree Rd
Kgn 10
@ 6:30 p.m.
CONTRIBUTION:
$700
For tickets or further information please contact 831-2006
www.facebook.com/praiseacademyofdanceja
Like
Comment

Vibes Time

With Anica Wood & Marlon Young

NUH WATCH NUH FACE

UNITY
Smartshag Photography
Praise Academy of Dance

BREAK FREE

LAUGHTER & JOY
Smartshag Photography

ENCOURAGEMENT

SIGNIFICANT IMPACT

PEACE

PEACE

PRIDE

ABANDONMENT

Praise Academy of Dance Presents
REGGAE VIBEZ
Covenant City Church, 72 Half Way Tree Road, Kgn
Saturday February 28, @ 7:00pm
FEATURING
PRAISE ACADEMY OF DANCE, LAUD DANCE MINISTRY
PORTMORE MISSIONARY DANCE MINISTRY
AND OTHERS.
Adults: $500.00 Children under 12: $300.00

Praise Academy of Dance Presents
REGGAE VIBEZ
An 18th ANNIVERSARY CELEBRATION,
"God Is Faithful"
Featuring Praise Jamaica, Praise Trinidad, Praise Barbados along with other Dance Ministries
March 5,2011
Venue: Stephanie Hall,
9 Skibo Avenue,Kgn.5
Time 6:30 pm
Contribution $500
Children age 3-12 $300
Proceeds in aid of The Inner City Boy's Dance Ministry (Lazarus) and our Junior Production "SCHOOLAS"
For more info contact Praise Academy of Dance Office/Studio(52A Molynes Road) Tel: 757-3326

Chapter 12

Watch the Feedback (Interviews)

1. Student A

Reggae music for me is an inspiration. I cannot study without listening to my gospel reggae music. It energizes me to overcome the challenges that I encounter from day to day.

I've been impacted by this genre of music during my journey as a young Christian. I was addicted to drugs and so strung out that I thought I would have lost my mind. This song by DJ Nicholas, "Cut It Off," enabled me to realise that God's love is unconditional and He doesn't write off anyone.

Growing up in a home where I had an absentee father, my life was a roller coaster because he left my mother with five siblings under twelve. I was the eldest and so I watched my mother's salty tears daily as she struggled to make ends meet. This was life in a rural community with no immediate access to light or water.

My early morning tasks were to seek water early so that all of us could have some tea and a little shower. I too felt lonely as I watched my mother and siblings go through hunger and pain, but my mother taught us how to pray.

Then one day a reggae song entitled "Pure Gold," by Prodigal Son and Rondel Positive, gave me a new perspective on life. We made a decision to allow God to help us through and He did. Today we can say that this type of music enables us to love our lives and serve God.

2. Student B

I was an abused child living in Majestic Gardens, with no love of either mother or father. My days were spent in isolation and other times with boys like me. We would steal, fight, speak swear words, hate other children who had the love of their parents. My behaviour at school was disgusting and uncaring, which led to me being suspended from school many times. But favour followed me although I didn't understand why.

One day Praise Academy of Dance along with Outreach Jamaica came on a mission to my community. They ministered this dance to the music "Woe" by Prodigal Son and it made me realise that God loves me.

3. New York

I'm not a Jamaican but a born New Yorker. I attended a dance conference where Praise Academy of Dance, Jamaica ministered in Dance to "Holy Ghost Church" by DJ Nicholas in an African Episcopal Church in Jamaica, New York. I was a reserved individual, very shy and uncomfortable around persons whom I had never met before.

I loved dancing but felt that the modern contemporary wasn't my style. So when I saw the ministry in reggae by Praise Academy I was instantly delivered. There was a recklessness and an abandonment in the movements that gave me hope to believe that movements are not limited to one genre of music. God is creative and if you believe that He can change your situation, He will, because He did it for me.

Chapter 13

Recommendations to the Ministry of Education, Youth & Culture

1. *Incorporation of gospel reggae music on the schools' curriculum beginning with Infant and Kindergarten through to High Schools*

End Results:

- Spiritually molded and grounded lives.
- Better adaptation to moral and holistic behavioural patterns and values.
- Positive attitudinal responses will flow through all aspects of their lives as they develop.
- Better environmental contributions and respect for law and order.

- Visual impact on families, homes, communities and nation.

2. *Development of Entrepreneurship Programmes and outlets for our youths to receive valid impartation to be role models and leaders in their communities.*

- This level of impartation will give our youths a better foundation from which to create a balance for a more sustainable future with successful benefits.

3. *Construction of Community Centres with high technology. This reflects a more versatile and creative way to have our youths who are not academically inclined surge into new territories to embrace this new passion.*

Through this new development our youths will be ably qualified to become young entrepreneurs and encourage others after them to change the environment in which they exist.

4. *Have more Christian and non-Christian investors from different companies see the importance of Reggae Gospel Music and dance as the bedrock of our nation and help to harness and embrace this venture.*

Conclusion

The words and chapters inscribed on the pages of this special nugget are written to unearth and activate the passion of a new sound and movement for the changing of not only a landscape, but the transformation of a life.

Isaiah 43:18-19 says:

"Forget the former things; do not dwell on the past. See I am doing a new thing! Now it springs up; do you not perceive it?

I am making a way in the wilderness and streams in the wasteland."

It's a scene you have never seen or experienced before. It comes with power and increased energy. This new sound and movement is ready to be launched with a different approach so that this generation does not lose sight of who our God is.

Joshua 1:7 says:

"Only be strong and very courageous, that you may observe to do according to all the law which Moses My servant commanded you; do not turn from it to the right hand or to the left, that you may prosper wherever you go."

These are uncharted territories that we have stepped in. So we refuse to be intimidated by naysayers or empty sounding, tinkling, negative voices. God knows exactly the path that He has chosen for this new venture and has already provided the tools and the human resources to accomplish this.

As we experience this new norm of LOCKDOWN in the COVID-19 pandemic, let's also see the positive elements that are evolving, especially for us as the 'Ecclesia'–the Church, the 'called out ones.' This time of reflection has enabled us to:

REPENT

REST

RESTORE

RECLAIM

It has allowed us to bring life to the dormant things, and to fulfil the lost nugget that is missing from the Church, which is worship involving the arts. Worship is not only singing, lifting of the hands, shouting and dancing. It is a lifestyle encompassing all of this and more. Being a lifestyle, it has become very casual and many of us have forgotten who Christ has called us to be. Although the pandemic has its negatives, there are positive elements and life stories which many of us can testify about that have given us a second chance at life.

So for those of us in whom God has deposited the different gifts and talents, it's a time to reflect, reinvent, strategise, and give worship to the Creator and not the gift. Repentance and total surrender is where it begins as we sharpen our tools for execution and revitalization.

This Hidden Nugget called gospel reggae music and dance is making its entrance into every heart of peoples in different nations. It cannot be hidden any longer because of its unique sound in quality, impact and the special and specific anointing and power that it carries.

Be ready to embrace and see the difference in your relationships both vertically with God and horizontally with the people you interface with daily, as you grow into this expression of fundamental change in an advancing creative world.

About the Author

Dr. Cynthia Patrica Noble was called into full-time Christian dance ministry in 1996, having previously taught academic subjects and dance for over 25 years in various primary and secondary schools in Jamaica, West Indies. She was subsequently ordained as a minister of dance in 2005 and served at the Portmore Lane Covenant Community Church as the head of the dance ministry. She is currently a member of the Fellowship Tabernacle, Portmore.

Cynthia Noble is a trained teacher and a graduate of Shortwood Teachers' College and holds a Diploma in Dance In Education from the Edna Manley College of the Visual and Performing Arts.

Cynthia, affectionately called 'Auntie Pat,' is the Founder of Praise Academy of Dance, Jamaica and Barbados. She is now retired and is continuing to utilise her gift of dance to train and develop younger dancers in churches and communities to identify their talents so they can bring transformation to both home and the community in which they live. Auntie Pat still sits on the board of Directors of the Praise Academy of Dance as a Dance Consultant.

She was honoured by the Greater Allen AME Cathedral of New York in 2008 at their 10th Anniversary GAC Worship Conference for being the pioneer of Christian dance in the Caribbean.

In October 2011, she was awarded the Bronze Musgrave Medal from the Institute of Jamaica for recognition of her contribution to the field of dance. She also received the Flame Award from the International Christian Dance Fellowship Foundation, based in Australia, in July 2012 for her outstanding service to Christian Dance Ministry on an international level.

In 2014 she received the Badge of Honour for Meritorious Service for contribution to culture in the area of Dance and Culture from the Governor General of Jamaica, Sir Patrick Allen.

In November 2018, she received the Honorary Degree of Doctor of Divinity from Grace Hill Bible College University in the State of New Jersey. This was for the work and ministry she fulfilled in Jamaica and other nations through Praise Academy of Dance, Jamaica.

Cynthia wrote her first book, entitled ***The Journey...Continues*** in 2014 which continues to impact many lives and ministries both locally and internationally. Her passion is to see the redemption of the dance and its restoration in every home, church and community as this new book, ***The Hidden Nugget Revealed***, is released.

It is her hope that this book will engage every child, teen and adult to allow Gospel Reggae and Dance to be the motivating factors for them to live by the word of God and daily apply it to their lives, so that their relationship with Christ can be firmly grounded.

Made in the USA
Middletown, DE
30 August 2024

59883435R00064